UNSTOPPABLE GOSPEL

GREGG MATTE

LifeWay Press® • Nashville, Tennessee

© 2016 LifeWay Press® • Reprinted 2016

ISBN 9781430053507 • Item 005784575

Dewey decimal classification: 226.6
Subject headings: CHURCH / BIBLE. N.T. ACTS—STUDY AND TEACHING / GOSPEL

Eric Geiger
Vice President, LifeWay Resources

Ronnie Floyd
General Editor

Gena Rogers
Sam O'Neal
Content Editors

Michael Kelley
Director, Groups Ministry

Send questions or comments to: Content Editor, *Bible Studies for Life: Adults;* One LifeWay Plaza; Nashville, TN 37234-0152; or make comments on the Web at *BibleStudiesforLife.com.*

Printed in the United States of America

To order additional copies of this resource, write to LifeWay Resources Customer Service; One LifeWay Plaza; Nashville, TN 37234-0113; fax 615.251.5933; email *orderentry@lifeway.com;* phone toll free 800.458.2772; order online at *lifeway.com;* or visit the LifeWay Christian Store serving you.

We believe that the Bible has God for its author; salvation for its end; and truth, without any mixture of error, for its matter and that all Scripture is totally true and trustworthy. To review LifeWay's doctrinal guideline, please visit *lifeway.com/doctrinalguideline.*

Scripture quotations are taken from the Holman Christian Standard Bible®, Copyright © 1999, 2000, 2002, 2003, 2009 by Holman Bible Publishers. Used by permission. Holman Christian Standard Bible®, Holman CSB®, and HCSB® are federally registered trademarks of Holman Bible Publishers.

Bible Studies for Life: Adults often lists websites that may be helpful to our readers. Our staff verifies each site's usefulness and appropriateness prior to publication. However, website content changes quickly, so we encourage you to approach all websites with caution. Make sure sites are still appropriate before sharing them with students, friends, and family.

contents

Social Media

Connect with a community of *Bible Studies for Life* users. Post responses to questions, share teaching ideas, and link to great blog content. ***Facebook.com/BibleStudiesForLife***

Get instant updates about new articles, giveaways, and more. **@BibleMeetsLife**

The App

Bible Studies for Life is also available as an eBook. The eBook can be opened and read with the *Bible Studies for Life App*, a free app from the iOS App Store or the Google Play Store.

Blog

At ***BibleStudiesForLife.com/blog*** you will find additional resources for your study experience, including music downloads provided by LifeWay Worship. Plus, leaders and group members alike will benefit from the blog posts written for people in every life stage—singles, parents, boomers, and senior adults—as well as media clips, connections between our study topics, current events, and much more.

Training

For helps on how to use Bible Studies for Life, tips on how to better lead groups, or additional ideas for leading this session, visit: ***ministrygrid.com/web/biblestudiesforlife.***

ABOUT THIS STUDY

Nothing stops our God. Nothing stops His gospel.

Don't write off the church.

Some people already have. They say they like Jesus, but there's no point to the church. As far as they're concerned, the church is a failed institution.

I disagree.

The church is far from a lost cause! In reality, the church is unstoppable because the followers of Christ have been given an unstoppable power—the very Spirit of God. Even more, they've been given an unstoppable mission and message.

Come with me on a journey through the exciting early days of the church. We'll discover what made the early church so powerful—so *unstoppable*. As the Book of Acts opens, we'll see a room full of huddled, scared disciples who were completely powerless and uncertain of the future. But we'll also see these same followers become empowered and effective men and women advancing throughout the world, proclaiming the unstoppable gospel that turned the world upside down.

The story of the unstoppable gospel continues today. It is our story as members of the church.

In Christ, we are unstoppable.

ABOUT THE AUTHOR

Gregg Matte

Gregg Matte is the senior pastor of Houston's First Baptist Church, a multi-site church with five campuses. Before coming to Houston's First in 2004, Gregg founded Breakaway Ministries at Texas A&M University, a weekly gathering that grew to more than 4,000 students.

Gregg is the author of *Unstoppable Gospel* (Baker Books, 2015), the book that is the basis for this study.

1 | UNSTOPPABLE MISSION

When has something definitely been worth the wait?

QUESTION #1

The Holy Spirit empowers us to spread the gospel.

THE BIBLE MEETS LIFE

We don't like to wait. Chalk it up to impatience, or maybe it's because we live in a world of instant gratification. But we want what we want when we want it.

▶ Two minutes waiting behind another customer at the fast food drive-thru? Too long.

▶ Sixty seconds to heat up food in a microwave? Too long.

▶ Fifteen seconds waiting for a movie to stream to your TV? Way too long!

At the end of His earthly ministry, Jesus told His disciples to wait. He was going to give them—and us—an incredible gift: the presence and power of His Holy Spirit. The disciples couldn't have fully appreciated what all that meant, but they waited nonetheless.

When the Holy Spirit came, He empowered Jesus' followers for a mission that was unstoppable. From that single location, their mission spread across the world—and continues today.

WHAT DOES THE BIBLE SAY?

Acts 1:4-5

⁴ While He was together with them, He commanded them not to leave Jerusalem, but to wait for the Father's promise. "This," He said, "is what you heard from Me; ⁵ for John baptized with water, but you will be baptized with the Holy Spirit not many days from now."

The life of a Christian is not hard; it's impossible. Following Jesus means:

▶ Loving people—even the people who hate you.

▶ Doing the ethical thing at work even it means putting your career on the line.

▶ Forgiving people who don't deserve to be forgiven.

The One who called us to this impossible life never sugarcoated how difficult it would be. In fact, Jesus said: "If anyone wants to come with Me, he must deny himself, take up his cross daily, and follow Me" (Luke 9:23). He also made this troubling promise: "You will have suffering in this world" (John 16:33).

Jesus, the Son of God, never expected us to live this impossible life in our own power. Indeed, Jesus Himself lived His life on earth in union with and empowered by the Holy Spirit. That same Spirit is the secret to the power we need to live and follow Jesus today. In other words, living the Christian life is only possible with the power of the Holy Spirit living through us.

In Acts 1:4-5, Jesus reminded His followers they soon would receive the gift He had promised earlier: the Holy Spirit. At Pentecost, the Spirit would descend on believers to empower them to preach the gospel. From that moment forward, God's people would be forever changed in how they related with Him.

What do you find difficult about waiting on the Lord?

QUESTION #2

Apart from the power of the Holy Spirit, we can do nothing of importance in our lives. But once we receive His power at salvation, we can do *anything* He calls us to do.

A little boy once heard that if he asked Jesus to be his Savior, God would come live inside his heart. So he asked his parents, "How can God live inside my heart? He's so big! He made the whole world! If He lived inside my heart, He'd stick out!"

That little boy was right. If God truly lives in our hearts, He's going to stick out. His love will stick out. His forgiveness will stick out. His power will stick out.

And the world will know.

Acts 1:6-8

⁶ So when they had come together, they asked Him, "Lord, are You restoring the kingdom to Israel at this time?" ⁷ He said to them, "It is not for you to know times or periods that the Father has set by His own authority. ⁸ But you will receive power when the Holy Spirit has come on you, and you will be My witnesses in Jerusalem, in all Judea and Samaria, and to the ends of the earth."

God sent the Holy Spirit to work through us to continue the work of bringing His children home. In verse 8, Jesus laid out God's agenda succinctly. His mandate in this verse laid the foundation for the rest of the Book of Acts, which is largely about how the early believers carried out this mandate.

Jesus told His followers to remain in Jerusalem and wait, because they would soon receive the power the Father had promised (see v. 4). When they were filled with the Spirit, they would be His "witnesses" telling what they had experienced with Jesus. They would do this with His power, not their own—the power of His Spirit.

> *What do these verses teach us about God's mission?*

QUESTION #3

BE MY WITNESSES

Use the space below to make a prayer list based on Acts 1:8. Fill out the different categories with specific requests you can echo throughout the coming week.

Lord, I'm praying this week that You do the following in my city:

_____

_____

Lord, I'm praying this week that You do the following in my nation:

_____

_____

Lord, I'm praying this week that You do the following in my world:

_____

_____

Lord, I'm praying this week that You do the following in my heart:

_____

_____

"He is no fool who gives what he cannot keep
to gain that which he cannot lose."

—JIM ELLIOT

The Greek word for "power" is *dunamis,* from which we get our English words "dynamo," "dynamite," and "dynamic." The Spirit empowers His church to do amazing things. By the power of the Holy Spirit, a tiny handful of believers turned the world upside down as the "gospel earthquake" rumbled from Jerusalem to the ends of the earth.

"Jerusalem … Judea and Samaria, and … the ends of the earth." Jesus laid out a deliberate plan of expansion that began at home and moved outward geographically to include all people. The same Spirit who descended on believers at Pentecost and turned the world upside down for Jesus is alive today in every person who has placed faith in Christ. He is sending you and me out on a mission.

▶ We can obey Acts 1:8 by hopping on a plane and flying to the ends of the earth.

▶ We can carry out Acts 1:8 by sending the good news out to the ends of the earth over the Internet.

▶ We can fulfill Acts 1:8 right at home, because the world is literally coming to our cities. Whenever you go to work, school, the store, or anywhere else in your town, you are likely to hear unfamiliar languages being spoken. We can carry the Lord's message to the ends of the earth in our own neighborhoods even as we also go to the ends of the earth.

We are empowered to be on mission to our city, nation, and world.

Acts 1:12-14

¹² Then they returned to Jerusalem from the mount called the Mount of Olives, which is near Jerusalem—a Sabbath day's journey away. ¹³ When they arrived, they went to the room upstairs where they were staying: Peter, John, James, Andrew, Philip, Thomas, Bartholomew, Matthew, James the son of Alphaeus, Simon the Zealot, and Judas the son of James. ¹⁴ All these were continually united in prayer, along with the women, including Mary the mother of Jesus, and His brothers.

What do you do when you find yourself waiting on the next thing God has for you? So many of us just try to stay busy. We fill the waiting with activity. Not these disciples. They went to a single upstairs room and *prayed*. In fact, they "were continually united in prayer" for ten days.

Let me share what I see in the disciples' ten-day prayer meeting:

▸ **Prayer is primary.** For many of us, prayer is often a last resort. "When all else fails, pray." But prayer was not the last resort for the early church. It was the main agenda.

▸ **Fear can be a great motivator.** For all the disciples knew, the same people who crucified their Lord might come for them, as well. It was fear, not piety, that drove the early church to its knees. In times of anxiety and fear, remember this: *If you go to your knees in fear, you'll rise up in faith.*

▸ **Prayer unites us.** The disciples "were continually united in prayer." They were single-minded, joined together as one. Why? Because prayer unites us.

Prayer maximizes "Thee" and minimizes "me." Prayer says, "My agenda is unimportant, Lord, but Your agenda is all-important." The reason for so much disunity and disharmony in the church is because many Christians contend for their own agendas, not God's agenda. When we pray and seek God's will together, He will unify us and keep us focused on our common center: Jesus the Lord.

> *What are some of the benefits of praying together as a group?*
>
> **QUESTION #4**

> *What common mission can our group pray for together?*
>
> **QUESTION #5**

LIVE IT OUT

Acts 1:8 is our mandate. It's mine, and it's yours. Therefore, consider taking one or more of the following steps toward fulfilling that mandate in the days to come:

▶ **Accept the mission.** Recognize that Jesus has commanded you to be His witness wherever you go and wherever He sends you. Verbally commit yourself to His service.

▶ **Embrace the gift.** Begin each day by submitting to the Holy Spirit as your only source of strength and guidance. Pray that He would give you wisdom and power to accomplish God's mission in your life.

▶ **Pray together.** Gather an extra time as a group this week. Make prayer the sole focus and action of that gathering.

God's mission is unstoppable—and so is the Spirit He's placed within you. Remember that you have a part to play in that mission. Remember also that it all begins with prayer.

My thoughts

2 | UNSTOPPABLE MESSAGE

What often gets you sidetracked during the day?

Jesus died for our sins, rose again, and reigns as Lord.

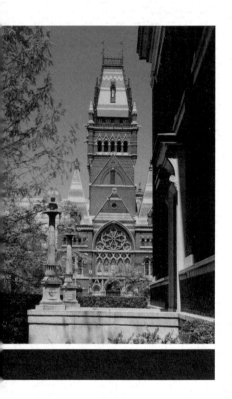

THE BIBLE MEETS LIFE

Do you know the original mission statement of Harvard University?

"Let every student be plainly instructed, and earnestly pressed to consider well, the main end of his life and studies is, to know God and Jesus Christ which is eternal life (John 17:3) and … seeing the Lord only giveth wisdom, let every one seriously set himself by prayer in secret to seek it of him (Prov. 2:3)."

Surprised? When the school was founded in 1636, the administration hired only Christian professors, the formation of Christian character was a top priority for students, and ministers were trained and equipped to share the gospel.

Today, Harvard maintains a legacy of academic excellence, but has lost its original mission—a phenomenon often described as "mission drift." The university lost sight of its original purpose.[1]

Unfortunately, mission drift happens in the church, as well. As we'll see in Acts 2, there is a clear, unstoppable message that drives our mission. It's up to us to stay the course.

WHAT DOES THE BIBLE SAY?

Acts 2:22-24

[22] **"Men of Israel, listen to these words: This Jesus the Nazarene was a man pointed out to you by God with miracles, wonders, and signs that God did among you through Him, just as you yourselves know.** [23] **Though He was delivered up according to God's determined plan and foreknowledge, you used lawless people to nail Him to a cross and kill Him.** [24] **God raised Him up, ending the pains of death, because it was not possible for Him to be held by it."**

Peter spoke of "God's determined plan," yet "lawless people" killed Him. In other words, God was in control, but the men involved were held responsible for their deeds. Peter stated these two truths together, unflinchingly and without apology.

As for human responsibility, we can never grasp the meaning of the cross until we understand the depth of our sin and how it separates us from God. Along with the lawless men who crucified Jesus, *we all are responsible for Jesus' death.* Once we see ourselves as sinners in need of salvation, we can understand why there had to be a cross—why the cross is vital to our message.

But Jesus didn't merely die; He rose again. If Jesus had sacrificed His life for us and then remained dead, His would be a poignant story about a martyr. But Jesus is unique in all of history. He is the only person who ever lived, died, and returned to life—never to die again. His death and resurrection are the heartbeat of the gospel message.

> *What can we learn from Peter's approach to sharing the gospel?*

QUESTION #2

Acts 2:32-33,36

[32] **"God has resurrected this Jesus. We are all witnesses of this. [33] Therefore, since He has been exalted to the right hand of God and has received from the Father the promised Holy Spirit, He has poured out what you both see and hear." ... [36] "Therefore let all the house of Israel know with certainty that God has made this Jesus, whom you crucified, both Lord and Messiah!"**

In A.D. 186, Polycarp, a church leader in Smyrna, stood before the Roman authorities and faced a decision. He could proclaim Caesar as lord and live, or he could refuse and die a martyr. For Polycarp, there was no other lord but Jesus. The proconsul weighed Polycarp's fate and urged him, "Swear, and I will release thee—reproach Christ."

But Polycarp held fast: "Eighty and six years have I served him, and he never once wronged me; how then shall I blaspheme my King, who hath saved me?" With that confession, Polycarp was burned alive and pierced with a sword. He died for professing his belief that Jesus alone is Lord.[2]

When the Romans called Caesar *kurius*, or "Lord," they were using that term in its highest sense: to signify divinity. They were acknowledging the emperor as their god, since the title denoted absolute sovereignty.

Peter used the same term at the climax of his sermon in Acts 2:36 to describe the absolute sovereignty of Jesus Christ: "'Therefore let all the house of Israel know with certainty that God has made this Jesus, whom you crucified, both Lord and Messiah!'" In this sense, *Lord* is a majestic title, used to show God's sovereignty and divine power. The word points to the Deity of Jesus; Peter was declaring Jesus is God.

Jesus "has been exalted to the right hand of God." With the Father, He sits in the most authoritative, sovereign position in the universe. It's because Jesus holds this most exalted position that He had the authority to pour out the Holy Spirit along with the signs and wonders people witnessed that day.

> **What are the personal implications of recognizing Jesus as Lord?**

QUESTION #3

Because Jesus is Lord and Messiah:

▶ **He is worthy of our worship.** He's not only worthy of our respect, but also of our worship. He is the One before whom every knee one day will bow (see Phil. 2:10-11).

▶ **He is worthy of our obedience.** Because Jesus is Lord and Messiah, He deserves to be sovereign in our lives. He has the absolute right to tell us what to do and expect our complete obedience.

> *What are the worldwide implications of Jesus' role as Lord?*

QUESTION #4

Acts 2:37-38

37 When they heard this, they came under deep conviction and said to Peter and the rest of the apostles: "Brothers, what must we do?" 38 "Repent," Peter said to them, "and be baptized, each of you, in the name of Jesus Christ for the forgiveness of your sins, and you will receive the gift of the Holy Spirit."

Peter's sermon had a devastating impact on his hearers. In the original Greek, Luke's words mean they were "cut to the heart." These people were suffering and sorrowing over the sin of having rejected and crucified the Messiah. They were filled with anguish and horror over what they had done.

The goal of biblical preaching is not to make people feel guilty or condemned, but to open their hearts to the conviction of the Holy Spirit. Here's why:

▶ **Condemnation** brings a general feeling of worthlessness, like a wet blanket. Condemnation leaves you feeling powerless and immobilized, totally discouraged from changing.

▶ **Conviction** brings awareness of specific sins, attitudes, and habits in your life that need to be changed. It's a specific spotlight on areas in need of care. When the Holy Spirit convicts you, He does so with the loving desire that you turn from sin and turn to Christ.

When the people asked, "What must we do?" Peter was poised and ready with a call to action: "Repent … and be baptized." The word *repent* in the Greek language means to change the way you think about your life and your behavior. It means agreeing that God is right and you are wrong. In essence, Peter told his listeners to repent and reverse the course of their lives.

Notice that baptism is a part of repentance. Peter was calling the crowd to be baptized *because* their sins had been forgiven. That's the unstoppable message: Jesus is Lord and Christ, and when we acknowledge Him and turn from our sin, we are forgiven.

> *As we share the gospel, how can we work toward the goal of conviction rather than condemnation?*

QUESTION #5

JESUS IS LORD

Use the space below to record words, phrases, or images that come to mind when you think of the word "Lord."

What are some practical steps you take to approach Jesus as Lord in your own life?

"If Jesus were born one thousand times in Bethlehem and not in me, then I would still be lost."

— CORRIE TEN BOOM

LIVE IT OUT

How will the unstoppable message of the gospel influence your life this week? Consider the following options:

▶ **Praise Him.** Jesus is worthy of our worship; therefore, set aside a time this week to praise Him in a way that is meaningful to you.

▶ **Share.** The message of salvation is for all Christians to share. Pray for opportunities to share the message of Jesus in your everyday conversations. Plan to tell someone this week about the difference Jesus has made in your life.

▶ **Invite others.** As you worship Jesus and share the truth of the gospel this week, invite others to join you. Find someone who needs a spiritually mature example and encourage him or her to join with you in following Jesus.

Let's avoid the dangers of "mission drift," both in our lives and in our churches. Let's not forget that the message of Jesus Christ and His salvation is the reason for everything we do.

My thoughts

1. Peter Greer and Chris Horst, *Mission Drift* (Bethany House, 2014), 17.
2. *http://www.ccel.org/f/foxe/martyrs/fox102.htm.*

What are some employee benefits that would get you excited?

THE BIBLE MEETS LIFE

Many businesses are famous not just for their products and services, but also for their work environments. For example:

▶ An Internet-related company offers its employees on-site vehicle maintenance, a laundromat, hair salon, and nap pods during work hours.

▶ A toy company offers paid time off for school-related absences like parent-teacher conferences or field trips.

▶ Other companies offer physical perks such as on-site gyms, pools, and even bowling alleys.[1]

These companies have created an inviting culture that draws people to work and keeps them happy.

The church is known for a culture that is far deeper than corporate perks. The early church's culture overflowed with love—love that reflected Jesus Christ and drew people to Him. Their example in Acts 2 challenges us to continue that reputation and be a church immersed in a culture of love.

WHAT DOES THE BIBLE SAY?

Acts 2:41-42

[41] So those who accepted his message were baptized, and that day about 3,000 people were added to them. [42] And they devoted themselves to the apostles' teaching, to the fellowship, to the breaking of bread, and to the prayers.

God did an incredible work in and through His people on the day of Pentecost. The Holy Spirit came upon the believers, Peter proclaimed the gospel of Jesus, and 3,000 people responded and were added to their number. Out of their common love for Christ, the believers came together and shared meals, worshiped and praised God together, and otherwise enjoyed one another's company. They continued to grow by learning under the apostles' teaching, fellowshipping together, and praying.

Let's focus for a moment on that crucial last element: *praying*.

Every great movement from God starts with prayer and is confirmed by prayer. As we saw in Acts 1, the first activity of the church was a prayer meeting.

What aspects of church life have been especially meaningful to you?

QUESTION #2

Prayer is the key to effective evangelism. We don't change people's hearts with our convincing arguments or clever presentations. Far more important than anything a believer can learn about evangelism is how much he or she depends on the Holy Spirit for witnessing. Before you start to have a conversation about Christ with your neighbor, coworker, or a fellow student—pause for prayer. It doesn't need to be a long, involved prayer. Sometimes it's enough to say, "Lord, let me speak Your words."

A friend of mine says, "The reason we don't pray is not because we're too busy, but because we're too confident." Jesus said, "You can do nothing without Me" (John 15:5); Paul wrote, "Pray constantly" (1 Thess. 5:17). Prayer should drive us to our knees in humility, knowing we need Jesus every hour.

Prayer allows God to change *me*—the one praying. As I pray in the love of Christ for others who don't know God, I become more burdened for their souls. As I pray for their broken relationships, health concerns, financial worries, or problems at work, I grow in concern and love for them. People will be more open to hearing our message when they sense that we genuinely care about them and what matters to them.

Praying for others leads to caring for others.

> **When have you seen the transformational power of prayer?**
>
> QUESTION #3

Acts 2:43-45

43 Then fear came over everyone, and many wonders and signs were being performed through the apostles. 44 Now all the believers were together and held all things in common. 45 They sold their possessions and property and distributed the proceeds to all, as anyone had a need.

The believers in the early church didn't just meet together to pray and worship. Verses 43-45 shows how they provided for one another's needs. Three characteristics are prominent:

▶ **Unity.** They "were together and held all things in common."

▶ **Selflessness.** "They sold their possessions and property."

▶ **Mutual care.** They "distributed the proceeds to all, as anyone had a need."

Caring for people is an incredible way to open a conversation about Jesus Christ. It's been said that people don't care how much you know until they know how much you care.

The first Christians were so committed to caring for others they sold their own possessions and property to provide for anyone among them who was in need. That's pretty radical. In the second century, a writer and philosopher named Aristides the Athenian described the early believers this way:

"They love one another: and from the widows they do not turn away their countenance: and they rescue the orphan from him who does him violence: and he who has gives to him who has not, without grudging. … And if there is among them a man that is poor or needy, and they have not an abundance of necessaries, they fast two or three days that they may supply the needy with their necessary food."[2]

Anything the early Christians contributed was a gift that came directly from the heart, not from autocratic rule. They gave from the overflow of their generosity.

Just as the early believers weren't required to sell all their possessions, neither are we. In this passage, Luke was describing what happened in the early church, not giving us a mandate. Nevertheless, their example of caring and extravagant love should motivate us to consider how we can imitate it.

How much should we give and how much should we keep? No one can give a pat, once-and-for-always answer to that question. We must find the balance in our own lives. The point is not to adopt an attitude of "How much do I *have* to give?" Rather, the point is to respond to the God who loves us extravagantly with a heart of loving generosity.

How would you describe a healthy balance between giving and keeping in today's world?

QUESTION #4

Acts 2:46-47

46 Every day they devoted themselves to meeting together in the temple complex, and broke bread from house to house. They ate their food with a joyful and humble attitude, 47 praising God and having favor with all the people. And every day the Lord added to them those who were being saved.

The early church certainly prayed and cared for others. But they didn't stop there. Perhaps if the believers had done only these two things, nothing more, none of us would know about Jesus today. At some point, in addition to praying for and helping people, they had to tell them about Jesus—who He is and why He lived, died, and rose again. They had to give voice to the message behind their loving acts.

In other words, the early believers evangelized! We know this is true because "every day the Lord added to them those who were being saved." This happened because someone who knew Jesus told someone who didn't know Jesus how to know Jesus.

In most situations today, the opportunity to share Christ is built on the foundation of friendship. You'll pray for a person and find some way to demonstrate you sincerely care—even if it's just to say, "I've been praying for you about that problem you shared with me." In the course of praying and caring, the Lord will give you an opportunity to share how Jesus is the answer to whatever he or she is going through.

Take a moment to think about these three simple acts: pray, care, and share. When we pray, God helps us to care for others. When we care, He leads us to share about His Son, Jesus. And the more we share the gospel, the more we are reminded to pray for those who need it.

Three simple acts become an incredible, dynamic lifestyle of loving God and serving others.

> *Loving others involves praying, caring, and sharing. In which of these areas would you like to grow?*

QUESTION #5

PRAY, CARE, SHARE

When will you pray for this person each day?

What's one practical step you can take in the coming week to show this person that you care?

What will you communicate to this person when an opportunity appears to share the good news of the gospel?

LIVE IT OUT

How will you actively and intentionally show love to people this week? Consider the following suggestions:

▶ **Pray.** Take a prayer walk through your neighborhood. Pray for the spiritual, emotional, and financial needs of each household—and pray especially for their salvation.

▶ **Care.** Actively look for someone in need this week. Determine to give sacrificially, whether of your time, money, or other resources to help that person in the name of Jesus.

▶ **Share.** Think of someone you've prayed for or helped in practical ways but never talked to about Jesus. Bring Jesus into your conversation with that person. Let him or her know your concern is motivated by the love of Christ in your life.

As members of the church, we have an opportunity to create a culture that's way more attractive than anything a corporation could produce. But it starts with you. Choose to pray, care, and share as a witness of Christ.

My thoughts

1. *http://www.businessinsider.com/company-perks-that-will-make-you-jealous-2014-7?op=1*
2. *The Apology of Aristides: on Behalf of the Christians*, edited by J. Rendel Harris (Wipf and Stock Publishers, 2004), 49.

When has a "chance" encounter changed your life?

QUESTION #1

#BSFLunstoppable

We intersect daily with people who need Christ.

THE BIBLE MEETS LIFE

In the early 70s, Bill Fernandez had two friends named Steve. Out walking around the neighborhood one afternoon with one of them, Bill saw the other Steve washing his car. It seemed like the perfect opportunity to introduce his two friends.

And that's how Steve Jobs and Steve Wozniak met. The two hit it off immediately, both having an avid interest in technology. Years later, the two Steves co-founded a little company called Apple®. A chance meeting led to the founding of one of the world's most highly valued businesses.[1]

Wait a minute. A *chance* meeting? As a follower of Christ, I hesitate to call the encounters I have with people mere "chance" meetings. These unplanned intersections can be "divine appointments"— opportunities that can change the direction of a life.

In Acts 3, Peter and John took advantage of just such an unplanned meeting to do something incredible for God.

WHAT DOES THE BIBLE SAY?

Acts 3:1-4

¹ **Now Peter and John were going up together to the temple complex at the hour of prayer at three in the afternoon. ² And a man who was lame from birth was carried there and placed every day at the temple gate called Beautiful, so he could beg from those entering the temple complex. ³ When he saw Peter and John about to enter the temple complex, he asked for help. ⁴ Peter, along with John, looked at him intently and said, "Look at us."**

Peter and John chose a busy intersection in Jerusalem. Three o'clock in the afternoon was one of the times designated daily for prayer; it was also the time for one of the two daily sacrifices. Therefore, it was a busy time at the temple with large crowds coming to pray and offer sacrifices. Peter and John likely chose this crowded time and place as a forum to share the gospel.

Before they started, Peter and John saw a disabled man begging from those who passed. This was similar to scenes we might see in urban America. I say we *might* see, because so many of us choose not to see. We walk on, avoiding eye contact.

Notice two truths from Peter and John's interaction with this lame beggar:

▶ **Individuals matter.** Peter and John had just seen 3,000 people come to Christ in one day, but they still saw and cared about an individual. They did just what Jesus did—they looked at the lame man as if, at that moment, no one else in the world mattered.

▶ **Intersections bring opportunity.** Just as we often drove through crossroads without really seeing what's there, we can also fail to notice the people we intersect with each day. God put us on this pathway called life, and we need to be aware of those who come and go in our lives.

How can we get better at noticing the opportunities God gives us to love others?

QUESTION #2

Up to this point, the beggar at the temple may have felt like no one ever noticed him. But no more. Peter said to him, "Look at us." Peter was acknowledging the man's presence and worth: "We see you. You are not invisible to us. We want to help."

Thanks to the willingness of Peter and John to turn a divine interruption into an unstoppable opportunity, this man's life was about to change. Forever.

Acts 3:5-8

5 So he turned to them, expecting to get something from them. 6 But Peter said, "I don't have silver or gold, but what I have, I give you: In the name of Jesus Christ the Nazarene, get up and walk!" 7 Then, taking him by the right hand he raised him up, and at once his feet and ankles became strong. 8 So he jumped up, stood, and started to walk, and he entered the temple complex with them—walking, leaping, and praising God.

There is an old Quaker proverb that states: "I expect to pass through this world but once. Any good therefore that I can do, or any kindness that I can show to any fellow creature, let me do it now. Let me not defer or neglect it, for I shall not pass this way again."

Those words reflect Peter and John's attitude toward the beggar. They didn't rationalize the way many people do when accosted by panhandlers: *I don't have any money. Someone else will help. He'll always be here begging. His relatives should provide for him. He should get a job.* Instead, Peter and John saw someone in need and viewed his need as an opportunity God had placed in their path.

"Peter said, 'I don't have silver or gold, but what I have, I give you: In the name of Jesus Christ the Nazarene, get up and walk!'" He took the disabled man by the right hand and pulled him to his feet. The man, who had been "lame from birth" (v. 2), may have expected to topple to the ground immediately; yet his feet and ankles supported him perfectly.

> **When have you seen Jesus make a dramatic difference in someone's life?**

QUESTION #3

COMMUNITY INTERSECTIONS

Use the space below to make a sketch or map of your community. Place an X on the main locations where different types of people gather on a regular basis.

How can your group use one or more of the locations above to create intersections with other people in your community?

"God needs no one,
but when faith is present
He works through anyone."

—A.W. TOZER

Think of the wild emotional ride the man surely must have experienced: disappointment when Peter told him he would receive no money; terror at being yanked to his feet; and finally, overwhelming joy when he was suddenly whole.

Think about these truths whenever you have a chance to give:

▶ **Peter and John gave what they had.** God always supplies what we need to do His work; otherwise, He wouldn't have brought us to that intersection. Even when we feel ill-equipped, we can take a step of faith.

▶ **Peter and John relied on Jesus.** The apostles didn't have the power to heal; Jesus did. When they said, "In the name of Jesus Christ the Nazarene, get up and walk," they were acknowledging the power and authority of Jesus to heal.

When we begin to open our eyes to the needs around us, it can be overwhelming. People in physical, emotional, and spiritual need are everywhere. Where do we begin—and how do we help with problems so deep-seated?

We must rely on the Holy Spirit to guide and empower us.

Acts 3:9-10

⁹ All the people saw him walking and praising God, ¹⁰ and they recognized that he was the one who used to sit and beg at the Beautiful Gate of the temple complex. So they were filled with awe and astonishment at what had happened to him.

The crowd responded with awe and astonishment. And why not? The man had been lame since birth. When a man has been unable to stand or walk for "over 40 years" (4:22), he just doesn't suddenly get better. So when the crowd saw this man standing, walking, and even leaping and praising God, it rightly got their attention!

If you read the rest of Acts 3, you'll see Peter grabbed this opportunity to talk about Jesus to all those who had come to the temple to worship. One opportunity to talk to one man about Jesus led to another opportunity. As a result, the number of the men alone who believed swelled to about 5,000 (see 4:4). It's the ripple effect: one opportunity leads to another. One changed life leads to another, and another.

Edward Kimball took an interest in a 17-year-old teenager and determined to reach out to him in the name of Jesus. In the shoe store where the young man worked, Kimball led Dwight L. Moody to faith in Christ. Moody would go on to lead thousands to faith in Christ, impacting a whole generation on two continents. Edward Kimball was an ordinary man, just like Peter and John—and just like us. God will take our little acts of obedience and multiply them a thousand times over.

One "yes" to the God-given opportunity in front of you can lead to ongoing impact. One "yes" can bring further opportunities. Because Peter and John responded to the man in their path, they had the opportunity to preach to a crowd. Multitudes responded, bringing more opportunities for ministry.

What does that mean for you? Say, "Yes."

> *How have you been affected personally by others' obedience to Christ?*
>
> **QUESTION #4**

> *How can we make room now so we can say yes to future opportunities to serve?*
>
> **QUESTION #5**

LIVE IT OUT

How will you make the most of the intersections and opportunities that come your way this week? Consider the following suggestions:

▶ **Look.** Search for such opportunities. Allow your schedule to be interrupted in order to minister by listening, offering encouragement, praying with someone, or meeting a need.

▶ **Go for it.** Take the steps of obedience that you've been putting off recently. Take a leap of faith and do what you know God has been calling you to do.

▶ **Sign up.** You don't have to wait for opportunities to fall in your lap through the regular intersections of life. Consider talking with a staff person at your church and signing up for ministry opportunities that match your gifts.

To follow Jesus is to serve a sovereign God—a God familiar with every nuance of your life and the lives of others. That doesn't leave much room for random chance. Therefore, be ready to respond when opportunities come your way.

My thoughts

1. *http://www.techrepublic.com/article/apples-first-employee-the-remarkable-odyssey-of-bill-fernandez/*

5 | UNSTOPPABLE COURAGE

> **What's the most courageous act you've ever seen?**

QUESTION #1

THE BIBLE MEETS LIFE

Most of us were taught as kids to "think before you speak." Sometimes, however, we need to speak even though we know our words will get us in trouble. That takes courage.

Consider Mathew Ayairga. The world reeled from the news in 2015 when 21 men from Egypt were kidnapped and beheaded because of their faith in Jesus Christ. Mathew was one of those kidnapped— but it turns out he was neither Egyptian nor a Christian. He just happened to be working in Libya with the other 20 men.

A transformation happened, though, on that fateful day. Kneeling on the beach with their executioners behind them, each man was commanded to renounce his faith, but each one died proclaiming Jesus Christ. When they came to Mathew and made the same demand, he said, "Their God is my God."[1]

Unstoppable courage. We see it first with Peter and John in Acts 4, and this unstoppable courage has continued on to others like Mathew Ayairga.

WHAT DOES THE BIBLE SAY?

Acts 4:1-3

¹ **Now as they were speaking to the people, the priests, the commander of the temple police, and the Sadducees confronted them,** ² **because they were provoked that they were teaching the people and proclaiming the resurrection from the dead, using Jesus as the example.** ³ **So they seized them and put them in custody until the next day, since it was already evening.**

As we saw in Acts 3, the miraculous healing of a lame man opened the door for Peter and John to speak about Jesus. Peter seized that opportunity to preach the gospel.

This was a change for Peter. When Jesus was arrested and put on trial, Peter had fearfully denied Him three times (see Luke 22:54-62). But now Peter was demonstrating the courage that failed him in those hours. Peter the Petrified became Peter the Passionate and Fearless.

In addition, Peter demonstrated unstoppable courage in front of the very same people who had terrified him before. Even as he was preaching about the Jewish leaders who had put their Messiah to death and how God had raised Him from the dead, guess who showed up?

▶ **The priests.** These were the ones in charge of operating the temple.

▶ **The commander of the temple police.** This man was essentially the chief of police.

▶ **The Sadducees.** This socially and politically powerful sect in Jewish society didn't believe in the resurrection from the dead. Luke noted they were upset by all the resurrection talk (see v. 2).

Jesus had said, "You will receive power when the Holy Spirit has come on you, and you will be My witnesses" (Acts 1:8). Peter now stood in that power and declared the gospel message without apology.

What are the risks we face when we proclaim the gospel?

QUESTION #2

The opposition Peter and John faced only showcased their courage. Courage is like a diamond on black velvet. It shines brightest against the darkest of circumstances. Courage always involves confrontation and the strong possibility of suffering. Courage is standing for Christ when you know you'll pay a price for doing so.

For Peter and John, the price was trouble with the authorities and a night in jail. This came as no surprise. Jesus had told them, "If they persecuted Me, they will also persecute you" (John 15:20).

We can expect confrontation when we speak for Jesus. But we can't let that silence us.

Acts 4:8-12

8 Then Peter was filled with the Holy Spirit and said to them, "Rulers of the people and elders: 9 If we are being examined today about a good deed done to a disabled man—by what means he was healed—10 let it be known to all of you and to all the people of Israel, that by the name of Jesus Christ the Nazarene—whom you crucified and whom God raised from the dead—by Him this man is standing here before you healthy. 11 This Jesus is the stone rejected by you builders, which has become the cornerstone. 12 There is salvation in no one else, for there is no other name under heaven given to people, and we must be saved by it."

The Jewish religious leaders asked a single question of Peter and John: "By what power or in what name have you done this?" (v. 7) They wanted to know how the lame man had been healed.

Peter had only one answer: Jesus.

Peter quoted Psalm 118:22, about the stone rejected by the builders becoming a cornerstone—but he referred to "the stone rejected by *you builders*" (emphasis added). They had executed their own Messiah. Peter went one step further with the truth: "There is salvation in no one else, for there is no other name under heaven given to people, and we must be saved by it."

PICTURING COURAGE

Which of the images below best represents your understanding of what it means to be courageous? Why?

   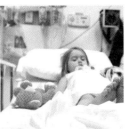

When have you needed courage in order to speak boldly for Christ?

"I believe it is a grave mistake to present Christianity as something charming and popular with no offense to it."

—DOROTHY SAYERS

Today, about half of all Americans believe there is more than one way to get to heaven. Among the other half—those who believe there is only one way to heaven—not all of them necessarily believe Jesus is that way. But even in the church, a staggeringly high number of Christians believe Jesus is not the only way to salvation.[2]

To claim as Peter did that "there is salvation in no one else" is a slap in the face of all those sincere people doing good and seeking God in other ways. That's intolerant!

Or is it? "Tolerance" should mean treating all people with respect, regardless of their beliefs. This definition has been altered, though, to mean accepting as *equally valid* all opinions and beliefs. It's been twisted into a relativistic moral code that says: "Neither of our beliefs is better or worse, right or wrong. Just different."

Biblical truth renounces this idea. Jesus Himself said, "I am the way, the truth, and the life. No one comes to the Father except through Me" (John 14:6). Among all the founders of the world's major religions, Jesus alone claimed to be God (see 10:30; 14:10-11). Only Jesus asserted that He had come to lay down His life for the sins of the world (see Mark 10:45). His resurrection from death validated His claims (see Matt. 12:38-42).

Peter laid the truth on the line about Jesus. Far from being intolerant, he spoke the truth in love.

In a culture that values tolerance above all, how do we boldly and lovingly communicate the message of verse 12?

QUESTION #3

How would you describe the role of the Holy Spirit in sharing the gospel?

QUESTION #4

Acts 4:19-20

¹⁹ But Peter and John answered them, "Whether it's right in the sight of God for us to listen to you rather than to God, you decide; ²⁰ for we are unable to stop speaking about what we have seen and heard."

Some people just can't admit they're wrong. The religious leaders had in front of them a once-crippled man standing on two strong legs. They were looking at a miracle, yet their hearts remained hard. They couldn't explain what Peter and John had accomplished, but they could make threats. By prohibiting Peter and John from speaking about Jesus (see v. 18), they were providing the basis to take further legal action should the apostles continue preaching the gospel.

Peter and John were ready with their courageous response: "We are unable to stop speaking about what we have seen and heard."

Christians today have an unhealthy need for others to like and approve of us. All too often, we are like the sign that reads: "I'm a recovering people pleaser—is that OK?" A healthy Christian outlook says:

▶ I don't serve to be validated. I serve because I am validated.

▶ I don't serve to be approved. I serve because I am approved.

▶ I don't serve because I'm insecure. I serve because I'm secure in Christ.

God's approval is all that matters. The opinions of others will come and go, but God's love is unchanging and unconditional. We can stand unwaveringly with Him. Why? Because He stood for us, He died for us, and He lives again. We are His.

The unstoppable gospel calls for unstoppable courage.

> *Where is God directing your group to demonstrate a greater level of courage?*

QUESTION #5

LIVE IT OUT

How will you demonstrate courage this week as you follow Christ? Consider the following suggestions:

▶ **Please God.** At the end of each day, evaluate your actions and attitudes by answering this question: "Whom did I live to please today?" Practice becoming a God-pleaser rather than a people-pleaser.

▶ **Read up.** Information is a great complement to courage. To better understand why Jesus is the only way to heaven, read *Jesus Among Other Gods: The Absolute Claims of the Christian Message* by Ravi Zacharias (W Publishing, 2002).

▶ **Take action.** Do some research and find a place in your community or state where the gospel is being silenced. Take action to get that policy changed: write to a government official, attend a public meeting and voice your opinion, start a petition, or join a group that works to correct the wrong.

Christians in America and other Western cultures are fortunate that we don't often find ourselves prohibited from sharing the gospel— nor do we find ourselves kneeling on a beach with guns pointed at us. Yet we can still demonstrate the unstoppable courage that has defined so many believers for so long. Will you?

My thoughts

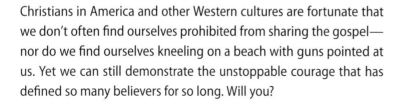

1. *http://www.persecution.com/public/newsroom.aspx?story_ID==373535*
2. *http://www.lifewayresearch.com/2014/10/28/americans-believe-in-heaven-hell-and-a-little-bit-of-heresy.*

6 | UNSTOPPABLE IMPACT

What do you enjoy most about different cultures?

QUESTION #1

#BSFLunstoppable

THE BIBLE MEETS LIFE

If you've ever visited another country, you know things are different.

▶ We've been taught it's rude to stick your tongue out at somebody, but in Tibet, that's a very polite gesture.

▶ We shake our heads when we mean "no," and nod our heads when we mean "yes." In Albania, those gestures are reversed.

▶ We like ketchup with our French fries, or perhaps a little mustard. The Dutch prefer mayonnaise.

Is one of these approaches better than another? No, just different. But even in this rich variety of preferences and styles, one truth is crucial in any cultural setting: the gospel of Jesus Christ. The gospel can speak into any culture—and does.

As the world becomes more diverse, we will encounter different cultures, ethnicities, worldviews, and preferences in everyday life. That's not a problem; it's an opportunity. We have a command to make disciples of all nations and an unstoppable gospel that can impact any culture for Jesus Christ.

WHAT DOES THE BIBLE SAY?

Acts 17:16-18

[16] **While Paul was waiting for them in Athens, his spirit was troubled within him when he saw that the city was full of idols.** [17] **So he reasoned in the synagogue with the Jews and with those who worshiped God and in the marketplace every day with those who happened to be there.** [18] **Then also, some of the Epicurean and Stoic philosophers argued with him. Some said, "What is this pseudo-intellectual trying to say?" Others replied, "He seems to be a preacher of foreign deities"—because he was telling the good news about Jesus and the Resurrection.**

Athens may have been the intellectual center of the world, but it was also a place of idolatry and superstition. Shrines and statues to Greek gods stood at the front door of every house, all around the marketplace, and even at street crossings. Athens alone may have held as many as 3,000 public statues and 30,000 idols. In *The Satyricon*, Roman satirist Petronius Arbiter, who lived at that time, wrote that it was easier to find a god than a man in that city.[1]

All this idol worship broke Paul's heart, but he chose to do something about it. He walked into the Agora—the marketplace—and sparked conversations. At the Agora he met two types of thinkers:

1. **Epicurean philosophers** believed the purpose of life was in finding pleasure and eliminating pain. They thought that God, if He existed at all, was not involved in our lives. Furthermore, they did not believe in life after death.

2. **Stoic philosophers** were pantheists, believing in an ultimate divine principle that exists throughout the universe and nature, including human beings. They believed the way to realize your fullest potential was to live by reason. The Stoics believed they could eliminate suffering through intellectual perfection.

What are the cultures and subcultures in your community?

QUESTION #2

Here in the cultural and intellectual center of the Roman Empire—where Plato, Socrates, and Aristotle had once taught, and where intellectuals still loved to debate—Paul dove right into the discussion with philosophers who were worlds apart from him in their beliefs. To be sure, these philosophers made fun of Paul, labeling him a "pseudo-intellectual." But Paul was not deterred.

When you know the truth and realize people need to hear it, you just engage, whatever the consequences.

Remember the words of Jesus: "No one lights a lamp and puts it under a basket, but rather on a lampstand, and it gives light for all who are in the house. In the same way, let your light shine before men, so that they may see your good works and give glory to your Father in heaven" (Matt. 5:15-16).

Acts 17:22-23

22 Then Paul stood in the middle of the Areopagus and said: "Men of Athens! I see that you are extremely religious in every respect. 23 For as I was passing through and observing the objects of your worship, I even found an altar on which was inscribed: TO AN UNKNOWN GOD. Therefore, what you worship in ignorance, this I proclaim to you."

When we meet someone different from us, we have a choice. We can focus on the differences and keep our distance, or we can find common ground and come together. We can build fences, or we can build bridges.

Paul was a bridge-builder.

When Paul talked about Jesus, some of the Stoic and Epicurean philosophers tagged him as a blowhard who didn't know what he was talking about. But others were intrigued. They wanted to hear more. So they escorted Paul to the Areopagus, the Athenian court and the hill where it convened, for a public hearing of sorts.

BUILDING BRIDGES

Paul used an important element of Athenian culture to build a bridge to the gospel. Choose two of the following elements of our culture and record how followers of Christ might build a bridge from that element to the gospel.

Movies

Sports

Reality TV

Music

Books

Video Games

"Then He said to them, 'Go into all the world and preach the gospel to the whole creation.'"

—MARK 16:15

Paul's audience didn't know about Jesus, nor did they believe in one God. Paul had no obvious connecting point to begin a conversation, but he found one: they worshiped, and so did Paul. Granted, they were worshiping the wrong things, but at least they were spiritual seekers. Paul used their spirituality to make a connection.

The construction of an altar "TO AN UNKNOWN GOD" was clearly the Athenians' attempt to make sure they didn't unintentionally forget, and thereby risk offending, one of the gods. Paul used their acknowledgment that there could be a god they didn't know as an opening to introduce them to "The God who made the world and everything in it" (v. 24). Moving forward, he proclaimed the truth about God and His plan to save them.

With the growing diversity in America, most of us rub shoulders daily with people who are very different from us. Separated by language, culture, religion, race, ethnicity, and politics, sometimes it's hard to find common ground. Yet, when you begin to look for a connecting point, you'll find it. Love of family, the pain of loss, hobbies and interests, food, work, health—these are things we all share.

Make it a point to look and listen for bridge-building material.

What principles and practices can we gain from Paul's approach to sharing the gospel?

QUESTION #3

Acts 17:30-31

³⁰ **"Therefore, having overlooked the times of ignorance, God now commands all people everywhere to repent, ³¹ because He has set a day when He is going to judge the world in righteousness by the Man He has appointed. He has provided proof of this to everyone by raising Him from the dead."**

It's great to go where people are and get involved in what they're doing. It's great to ask questions and start discussions. But it doesn't end there. To stop there is like walking away from the marathon just short of the finish line.

Why are so many Christians comfortable with remaining silent?

QUESTION #4

During the days of Elisha, the Arameans were at war with Israel. The city of Samaria was under siege and food was scarce (see 2 Kings 6:8,24-29). One day, four lepers, living outside the city because of their disease, decided to go to the Arameans in hopes of finding food. To their astonishment, the Aramean camp was a ghost town. During the night, the Lord had caused the Arameans to flee. They left behind food, clothing, silver, and gold. The four lepers had escaped their dire straits and landed in paradise.

The lepers ate and drank their fill and hid their plunder (see 7:5-7). Then they remembered their kinsmen starving back in the city. "Then they said to each other, 'We're not doing what is right. Today is a day of good news. If we are silent and wait until morning light, our sin will catch up with us. *Let's go tell the king's household'*" (v. 9, emphasis added).

Those of us who know Jesus are a lot like those lepers who found hope. We have found the answer to our deepest need, but it's also the answer to the deepest needs of all those people "back in the city" who don't yet know Jesus as Savior. This is a day of good news! The gospel is too good not to share.

As Paul spoke at the Areopagus, he couched the message in terms familiar to his listeners. He quoted their poets and spoke their language. But he still got down to the gospel. The Athenians struggled to accept God as Creator and Judge and to believe in Jesus' resurrection, but on these points, Paul did not compromise the truths of the gospel.

Paul met them on their grounds, brought the truth of Jesus into the conversation, and crossed the finish line in communicating the gospel. The rest was up to God.

How can our group engage one or more of the cultures in our community?

QUESTION #5

LIVE IT OUT

We have an imperative to take the gospel to the world, but the nations have also come to us. Therefore:

▶ **Get educated.** Learn about the different cultures of the people in your community. Ask about their customs, heritage, and beliefs. Attend an ethnic festival or performance. Become a student of different cultures in an effort to start discussions.

▶ **Get spiritual.** Follow Paul's example by attending a worship service within a different culture. Seek out common ground in order to build bridges between that culture and Christ.

▶ **Get official.** Talk with a staff person at your church about forming a ministry outreach to serve the different cultures in your community.

Yes, things are different in other countries and in other cultures. Those differences are neither bad nor good, yet they present a wonderful opportunity to share the good news about Jesus.

My thoughts

1. Petronius Arbiter, *The Satyricon,* translated by W. C. Firebaugh, Chapter 17.

My group's prayer requests

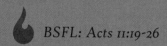
WHEN GOD SCATTERED HIS WITNESSES

BY GREGORY T. POUNCEY
EXCERPTED FROM *BIBLICAL ILLUSTRATOR*

TERTULLIAN, A SECOND-CENTURY THEOLOGIAN, referred to the blood of the martyrs as being the seed of the church. [1] By this, he meant to demonstrate that every time the church experienced persecution, it also grew in number and spirit. This phenomenon did not begin with Tertullian's time. From the moment the church began to experience persecution, it began to grow stronger both spiritually and numerically.

Jewish leaders stoned Stephen to death (see Acts 7:54-60). Afterward, Jewish persecution against the Christians intensified. As a result, many Hellenistic Christians opted to flee to other parts of the empire to live out their faith rather than remain in Jerusalem. Not only Hellenistic Christians but Hellenistic Jewish Christians scattered from Jerusalem to other parts of the Roman Empire (see 8:1,4). Acts 11:19-26 describes the growth that occurred as a result of this persecution and scattering.

The earliest Christians did not considered themselves to be followers of a new religion; they saw their faith in Christ as an extension of the Jewish faith. They continued practicing Judaism— believing they had lived to see the messianic age. [2] For a brief time, this coexistence did not necessitate a split in the two religions, for even the Roman world looked at them as being the same faith. However, as the Christian community began to understand the Old Testament in light of Jesus being the Messiah and as the pagan world began to oppose Christianity, the Jewish community felt the need to distance themselves from the new movement. The aftermath of Stephen's stoning was the impetus to this dispersion of Christians from Jerusalem, and it profoundly affected the new movement of Christ followers.

Historian Robert Baker said, "The martyrdom of Stephen marks a turning point in two respects: it began the persecution that drove the Christians out of Jerusalem into all Judea and Samaria in their witness; and it profoundly moved Saul the persecutor in the direction of personal conversion to Christ." [3] Certainly these two turning points profoundly shaped Christianity's future, but how? The scattering of the church decentralized the church, shifted the emphasis to reaching the Gentiles, and propelled the missions movement of the church.

Decentralized the Church

The early church had a great respect for the apostles, as they should have. These were the men who walked with Jesus and learned directly from Him. Even hundreds of years later when the church made decisions about which books should appear in the canon, apostolic authority carried the day for many books. [4] Apostolic authority and leadership were crucial for the budding church. As long as they were alive, the apostles could be a final voice for church questions. Those who followed them, however, did not have the same authority and could not offer the same leadership. The scattering of the church, therefore, began the process of decentralizing the church where one region of the church did not have authority over another.

In Acts 15, a dispute arose about Gentiles who had become Christians. The most heated debate centered on circumcision (see v. 1). Some believed that those who did not submit to circumcision could not be saved. Because the church had scattered to different places, the leaders in Jerusalem tried to determine a policy that would serve the church in its various locations (see v. 6). The Jerusalem church still remained a powerful and authoritative voice for all Christians who had scattered, yet they sent a letter of recommendation rather than a mandate back to the churches. The Jerusalem Council agreed circumcision was unnecessary for the Gentiles, but they instructed the new Christians to be mindful of things that would offend Jewish Christians and to remain morally pure (see v. 29).

In time, the emphasis on the Jerusalem church began to wane. Herod Agrippa ordered the death of James, John's brother (see 12:1-2). He arrested Simon Peter and may have attempted to martyr him, but God divinely released Peter (see vv. 3-19). In A.D. 62, James, the brother of Jesus, faced martyrdom at the hands of the high priest. [5] Finally, with the destruction of the temple in A.D. 70, the dominance that the Jerusalem church had over the scattered church diminished.

Shifted the Emphasis to Reaching Gentiles

A second turning point with the scattering of the church was a desire to reach Gentiles. Certainly this had already begun through Simon Peter's ministry to Cornelius (see 10:44-48). This, though, was a Jewish man reaching a Gentile on Jewish soil (Caesarea). As the Jewish Christians scattered to other parts of the empire, they encountered Gentiles who also needed Christ. Immediately after the scattering that resulted from Stephen's martyrdom, Luke mentioned Philip's ministry in Samaria and the Ethiopian eunuch's conversion (see 8:4-8,26-40). Likewise, as Hellenistic Christians scattered to new locations, they spread the gospel to the Gentiles. Indeed, "God…granted repentance resulting in life to even the Gentiles!" (11:18).

ILLUSTRATOR PHOTO/ BRENT BRUCE (60/0167)

ILLUSTRATOR PHOTO/ BOB SCHATZ/ ROYAL ONTARIO MUSEUM, TORONTO (29/12/17)

Above: The so-called Tomb of St. James in the Kidron Valley, east of Jerusalem.

Left: The James Ossuary, which has been the subject of both scholarly debate and legal action. The disagreements question the authenticity of the inscription, which reads: "James son of Joseph, brother of Jesus."

This emphasis on preaching to the Gentiles spread to the believers that had settled in Antioch (see vv. 19-26). The context of this passage indicates two men, one from Cyprus and one from Cyrene, had come from the Hellenists in Jerusalem and preached the gospel to Gentiles. [6] Luke described their effect as, "The Lord's hand was with them, and a large number who believed turned to the Lord" (v. 21). As believers scattered, they carried with them a newfound interest in reaching Gentiles.

Propelled the Missions Movement of the Church

A final result of the scattering of the early church was an interest in sending mission teams to reach other places of the world. Apparently, in each city where Christians scattered, they founded churches and raised up in them maturing believers who would serve as leaders in the local church (see 13:1). The churches functioned autonomously, even though at certain points, such as the decision about circumcision in Acts 15, they wanted to seek the approval of the Jerusalem church. As the Jerusalem church's authority waned, as mentioned above, each individual church began to function as its own entity.

As the church in Antioch gathered for worship, God placed on their hearts a desire to send missionaries to other parts of the Roman Empire. The Lord singled out Barnabas and Saul for this task in the beginning (see 13:2-3). Until this point, the church grew as it scattered. However, the scattered church

saw the need, through the leading of the Spirit, to become more intentional in their attempts to spread the gospel. The first mission team went to Cyprus and cities in Galatia, and then returned to Antioch to share the results of their journey. Thus, the scattered church in Antioch had become a sending agency for missions.

Though Barnabas and Saul were the first missionaries to leave the scattered churches, "The missionary task itself was undertaken, not only by Paul and others whose names are known—Barnabas, Mark, et al.—but also by countless and nameless Christians who went from place to place taking with them their faith and their witness." [7] Though Paul first would enter the synagogues and preach the gospel to the

ILLUSTRATOR PHOTO/ BOB SCHATZ (25/3/13)

ILLUSTRATOR PHOTO/ BOB SCHATZ (8/42/3)

Above: Interior of the rock-carved Church of St. Peter in Antioch (modern Antakya, Turkey).

Right: The Lion Gate at the old city of Jerusalem. This is also called Saint Stephen's Gate, as tradition holds that Stephen was stoned in this region.

Left: Interior of the Church of Ananias, which is just off of the Street called Straight in Damascus. After his conversion, Paul went to the house of Ananias in Damascus, where the Lord restored his sight.

Thus, the scattered believers shifted the early church's focus from Jerusalem to the world. The persecution the early church in Jerusalem experienced proved to be beneficial. The church moved from embracing a provincial message intended for one people to proclaiming a worldwide faith that needed to be shared with all. Jesus had not come for the Jews alone, but for the whole world (see John 3:16).

1. Tim Dowley, Org. Ed., *The History of Christianity* (Bristol, Great Britain: Lion Publishing, 1977), 84.
2. Justo L. Gonzalez, *The Story of Christianity*, vol. 1 (New York: Harper Collins, 1984), 20.
3. Robert A. Baker, *A Summary of Christian History* (Nashville: Broadman Press, 1959), 9.
4. F.F. Bruce, *The Canon of Scripture* (Downers Grove, IL: InterVarsity Press, 1988), 256.
5. Gonzalez, 21.
6. Kenneth O. Gangel, *Acts*, vol. 5 in *Holman New Testament Commentary* (Nashville: Holman Reference, 1998), 179. Gangel states, "Instead of returning home, they headed north to Antioch." When they scattered, they probably left with the intention of preaching the gospel wherever they went.
7. Gonzalez, 25.

Jews, he also made a considerable effort to preach to the Gentiles as well. Acts 13:46 emphasized the shift, "Then Paul and Barnabas boldly said: 'It was necessary that God's message be spoken to you first. But since you reject it and consider yourselves unworthy of eternal life, we now turn to the Gentiles!'"

Want to know more about Bible backgrounds, culture, history, archaeology, cities, persons — and other related topics? *Biblical Illustrator* is the magazine for you. For further information or to order your copy, go to: *lifeway.com/biblicalillustrator*.

LEADER GUIDE | UNSTOPPABLE GOSPEL

GENERAL INSTRUCTIONS

In order to make the most of this study and to ensure a richer group experience, it's recommended that all group participants read through the teaching and discussion content in full before each group meeting. As a leader, it is also a good idea for you to be familiar with this content and prepared to summarize it for your group members as you move through the material each week.

Each session of the Bible study is made up of three sections:

1. THE BIBLE MEETS LIFE.

An introduction to the theme of the session and its connection to everyday life, along with a brief overview of the primary Scripture text. This section also includes an icebreaker question or activity.

2. WHAT DOES THE BIBLE SAY?

This comprises the bulk of each session and includes the primary Scripture text along with explanations for key words and ideas within that text. This section also includes most of the content designed to produce and maintain discussion within the group.

3. LIVE IT OUT.

The final section focuses on application, using bulleted summary statements to answer the question, *So what?* As the leader, be prepared to challenge the group to apply what they learned during the discussion by transforming it into action throughout the week.

For group leaders, the *Unstoppable Gospel* Leader Guide contains several features and tools designed to help you lead participants through the material provided.

QUESTION 1—ICEBREAKER

These opening questions and/or activities are designed to help participants transition into the study and begin engaging the primary themes to be discussed. Be sure everyone has a chance to speak, but maintain a low-pressure environment.

DISCUSSION QUESTIONS

Each "What Does the Bible Say?" section features six questions designed to spark discussion and interaction within your group. These questions encourage critical thinking, so be sure to allow a period of silence for participants to process the question and form an answer.

The *Unstoppable Gospel* Leader Guide also contains follow-up questions and optional activities that may be helpful to your group, if time permits.

DVD CONTENT

Each video features Gregg Matte discussing the primary themes found in the session. We recommend you show this video in one of three places: (1) At the beginning of the group time, (2) After the icebreaker, or (3) After a quick review and/or summary of "What Does the Bible Say?" A video summary is included as well. You may choose to use this summary as background preparation to help you guide the group.

The Leader Guide contains additional questions to help unpack the video and transition into the discussion. For a digital Leader Guide with commentary, see the "Leader Tools" folder on the DVD-ROM in your Leader Kit.

For helps on how to use *Bible Studies for Life,* tips on how to better lead groups, or additional ideas for leading, visit: *ministrygrid.com/web/BibleStudiesforLife.*

SESSION 1: UNSTOPPABLE MISSION

The Point: The Holy Spirit empowers us to spread the gospel.

The Passage: Acts 1:4-8,12-14

The Setting: After Jesus rose from the dead, for 40 days He appeared to His disciples, showing Himself to be alive and instructing them on the kingdom of God (see Acts 1:3). Although He was preparing to return to God the Father, as He had promised, the disciples would not be left alone. They would receive "the Father's promise," the Holy Spirit, who would be with them to teach them and empower them. As the time arrived for Jesus to leave His disciples, He spoke with them one last time.

QUESTION 1: When has something definitely been worth the wait?

> *Optional activity:* Prior to discussing Question 1, give group members a small taste of what it feels like to wait. At the normal start time for your gathering, excuse yourself and leave the room for 3-5 minutes. When you return, announce that you wanted to give everyone a chance to experience waiting in real-time before discussing Question 1. Ask what people thought and felt while they were waiting for you to return.

Video Summary: God does something amazing in the early church. We see Him use ordinary people in extraordinary ways. And in doing so, He sets in motion a trajectory that allows us to experience some of those same things today. In Acts 1, we see that the church had to wait. And what they did while they were waiting is very important—they prayed. Just as with the early church, God has a purpose in our waiting. He is doing something *in* us so that He can do something *through* us.

▶ WATCH THE DVD SEGMENT FOR SESSION 1. THEN USE THE FOLLOWING QUESTIONS AND DISCUSSION POINTS TO TRANSITION INTO THE STUDY.

- Greg talks about the correct order of action while we wait—pray, plan, then proceed. How do you usually react when you are required to wait?
- What actions can you take to make your wait more meaningful?

WHAT DOES THE BIBLE SAY?

▶ ASK FOR A VOLUNTEER TO READ ALOUD ACTS 1:4-8,12-14.

Response: What's your initial reaction to these verses?

- What do you like about the text?
- What questions do you have about these verses?

► TURN THE GROUP'S ATTENTION TO ACTS 1:4-5.

QUESTION 2: What do you find difficult about waiting on the Lord?

Answering this question requires group members to examine the times in their own lives when they have found it difficult to wait on the Lord and why that has been the case. Remind them that they are not alone and encourage them in their honesty. Since this question is more personal in nature, consider starting the discussion by sharing your own experience.

> ***Optional follow-up:*** When have you anticipated God working in a specific way?

► MOVE TO ACTS 1:6-8.

QUESTION 3: What do these verses teach us about God's mission?

This question asks group members to interpret the biblical text in terms of what can be learned from this passage about God's mission. Encourage them to look beyond the words.

> ***Optional activity:*** Direct group members to complete the activity "Be My Witnesses" on page 11. If time permits, encourage volunteers to share their responses.

► CONTINUE WITH ACTS 1:12-14.

QUESTION 4: What are some of the benefits of praying together as a group?

This question calls for application based on the biblical text and is designed to help group members identify benefits of praying as a group. Encourage them to be specific in their responses.

> ***Optional follow-up:*** What circumstances can cause us to doubt we have God's power within us?

QUESTION 5: What common mission can our group pray for together?

This is an application question designed to promote biblical community. Guide group members to respond with actions you can take as a group, not as individuals.

> ***Optional follow-up:*** How is praying with others for a common mission different from your own personal prayers?

Note: The following question does not appear in the group member book. Use it in your group discussion as time allows.

QUESTION 6: What is our role in accessing the Holy Spirit's power as witnesses for Christ?

This question provides an opportunity for group members to interpret and internalize the biblical text to determine their role and responsibility in sharing the gospel. Consider opening discussion of this question by drawing attention back to the point of this session.

LIVE IT OUT

Acts 1:8 is our mandate. Encourage group members to consider taking one or more of the following steps toward fulfilling that mandate in the days to come:

- **Accept the mission.** Recognize that Jesus has commanded you to be His witness wherever you go and wherever He sends you. Verbally commit yourself to His service.

- **Embrace the gift.** Begin each day by submitting to the Holy Spirit as your only source of strength and guidance. Pray that He would give you wisdom and power to accomplish God's mission in your life.

- **Pray together.** Gather an extra time as a group this week. Make prayer the sole focus and action of that gathering.

Challenge: God's mission is unstoppable—and so is the Spirit He's placed within you. Remember that you have a part to play in that mission, and it all begins with prayer. Spend some extra time every morning this week asking the Lord to make you constantly aware of opportunities He is placing before you to live out Acts 1:8.

Pray: Ask for prayer requests and ask group members to pray for the different requests as intercessors. As the leader, close this time by thanking God for His work in and through the church over the course of centuries. Declare your desire to participate in the church's unstoppable mission.

SESSION 2: UNSTOPPABLE MESSAGE

The Point: Jesus died for our sins, rose again, and reigns as Lord.

The Passage: Acts 2:22-24,32-33,36-38

The Setting: After Jesus' ascension, the disciples followed His command to return to Jerusalem to await the coming of the Holy Spirit. Gathered together on the Day of Pentecost, the Holy Spirit descended upon them with the sound of a violent rushing wind and the appearance of flames, like tongues of fire. The disciples began to speak in different languages, which the Jews gathered for Pentecost from the various nations could comprehend in their own languages (see Acts 2:1-6). The crowd was amazed, and Peter took this opportunity to tell them about Jesus and the good news of the gospel.

QUESTION 1: What often gets you sidetracked during the day?

> *Optional activity:* As a supplement to "The Bible Meets Life," ask group members to identify the main goal or message of the following organizations. You can also encourage group members to share companies or organizations they feel have done a good job of staying focused on their message for a long period of time.
> - Apple®
> - The United Nations
> - The Red Cross
> - The Environmental Protection Agency
> - The Church

Video Summary: Acts 2 contains the first sermon ever preached. After Jesus' ascension, the disciples followed His command to return to Jerusalem to await the coming of the Holy Spirit. Gathered together on the Day of Pentecost, Peter took the opportunity to tell them about Jesus and the good news of the gospel. The message of the church today is the same. And the message of Jesus is for everyone. We get messages from lots of different places—television, radio, social media. We can be tempted to communicate our own message and maybe sprinkle a little Jesus on it. But the central message for believers is Christ. And this message should come through every aspect of our lives.

▶ WATCH THE DVD SEGMENT FOR SESSION 2. THEN USE THE FOLLOWING QUESTIONS AND DISCUSSION POINTS TO TRANSITION INTO THE STUDY.

> - In what ways do your day-to-day actions communicate the true message of your life?
> - If someone new walked into your group, what do you think they would see as the message of your group?

WHAT DOES THE BIBLE SAY?

▶ ASK FOR A VOLUNTEER TO READ ALOUD ACTS 2:22-24,32-33,36-38.

Response: What's your initial reaction to these verses?

- What questions do you have about these verses?
- What do you hope to learn this week about the message of Christ?

▶ TURN THE GROUP'S ATTENTION TO ACTS 2:22-24.

QUESTION 2: What can we learn from Peter's approach to sharing the gospel?

This question is designed to help group members actively engage the Scripture text and then interpret and apply what they can learn personally from Peter through the lens of this passage.

Optional follow-up: What are the essentials of the gospel message?

▶ MOVE TO ACTS 2:32-33,36.

QUESTION 3: What are the personal implications of recognizing Jesus as Lord?

Again, this passage allows group members an opportunity to apply Scripture to their daily lives through the interpretation of the biblical text.

Optional follow-up: When is it a struggle to know with certainty that Jesus is Lord?

QUESTION 4: What are the worldwide implications of Jesus' role as Lord?

This question requires group members to respond based on a broad perspective of what Jesus' power means on a worldwide scale. As time permits, consider bringing the discussion back to the implications of His power for group members in their day-to-day.

▶ CONTINUE WITH ACTS 2:37-38.

QUESTION 5: As we share the gospel, how can we work toward the goal of conviction rather than condemnation?

This question is designed to give group members an opportunity to define for themselves two terms that not only influence their understanding of the gospel but impact how they communicate this important message to others.

Optional activity: Direct group members to complete the activity "Jesus Is Lord" on page 21. If time permits, encourage volunteers to share what comes to mind when they think of the word "Lord."

Note: The following question does not appear in the group member book. Use it in your group discussion as time allows.

QUESTION 6: How did you initially respond when you first heard the gospel?

This question invites members of the group to share their personal testimonies of how they first responded to the good news of the gospel. Answers will vary based on experience. Encourage group members to be honest.

> **Optional follow-up:** In what ways might your initial reaction to the gospel better prepare and equip you to share with others who have never heard?

LIVE IT OUT

How will the unstoppable message of the gospel influence your life this week? Invite group members to consider the following options:

- **Praise Him.** Jesus is worthy of our worship; therefore, set aside a time this week to praise Him in a way that is meaningful to you.

- **Share.** The message of salvation is for all Christians to share. Pray for opportunities to share the message of Jesus in your everyday conversations. Plan to tell someone this week about the difference Jesus has made in your life.

- **Invite others.** As you worship Jesus and share the truth of the gospel this week, invite others to join you. Find someone who needs a spiritually mature example and encourage him or her to join with you in following Jesus.

Challenge: The message of Jesus Christ and His salvation is the reason for everything we do. To help you maintain your focus this week, consider keeping a list of the times you recognize you are experiencing "mission drift." Re-examining this list later will give you better perspective of the things that most easily get you off track.

Pray: Ask for prayer requests and ask group members to pray for the different requests as intercessors. As the leader, conclude by praising God for the simplicity of the gospel message. Ask for opportunities to share that message throughout the coming week, and ask for the courage to take advantage of those opportunities when they come.

SESSION 3: UNSTOPPABLE LOVE

The Point: Loving people is a powerful expression of loving God.

The Passage: Acts 2:41-47

The Setting: On the Day of Pentecost, the Holy Spirit descended upon the disciples of Jesus. Empowered by the Spirit to speak to the Jews present in Jerusalem for Pentecost in their own languages, the people were amazed and Peter preached to them, telling them about Jesus and the good news of the gospel. Acts 2:41-47 details that about 3,000 people believed after Peter's sermon and describes the growth of the early church.

QUESTION 1: What are some employee benefits that would get you excited?

> *Optional activity:* If possible, bring in a white board or tear sheets to record the different ideas people present. After everyone has shared their ideas, take a series of votes to determine which employee benefit would be considered most appealing by your group.

Video Summary: Unstoppable love creates opportunities to share the gospel. But we need to be in prayer for people before we tell them about Christ. Praying for others leads to a genuine care for them. Prayer builds relationship, and prayer births love for each other and for Christ. Out of their common love for Jesus, we can express an unstoppable love for each other that comes from a resource greater than ourselves. It comes from the Holy Spirit.

▶ WATCH THE DVD SEGMENT FOR SESSION 3. THEN USE THE FOLLOWING QUESTIONS AND DISCUSSION POINTS TO TRANSITION INTO THE STUDY.

- In what ways do you feel your love for others displays your love for God?
- How does this differ from how you want to be known?

WHAT DOES THE BIBLE SAY?

▶ ASK FOR A VOLUNTEER TO READ ALOUD ACTS 2:41-47.

Response: What's your initial reaction to these verses?

- What questions do you have about these verses?
- What new application do you hope to get from this passage?

▶ TURN THE GROUP'S ATTENTION TO ACTS 2:41-42.

QUESTION 2: What aspects of church life have been especially meaningful to you?

This question provides group members with an opportunity to share from personal experience by requiring them to really focus on the aspects of church life that mean the most to them.

> **Optional follow-up:** In what ways could you use these things to share the love of God with others? Be specific.

QUESTION 3: When have you seen the transformational power of prayer?

Through sharing a personal story group members will be required to define for themselves what the transformational power of prayer looks like.

> **Optional follow-up:** What are some words that describe your experience with prayer?

▶ MOVE TO ACTS 2:43-45.

QUESTION 4: How would you describe a healthy balance between giving and keeping in today's world?

Consider discussing this question as a group rather than individuals. Encourage group members to brainstorm specific ways to find a healthy balance between giving and keeping. Remind them to listen closely for what they can learn from others in the group.

> **Optional follow-up:** What would it look like for our group to practice the extravagant love we see in this passage?

▶ CONTINUE WITH ACTS 2:46-47.

QUESTION 5: Loving others involves praying, caring, and sharing. In which of these areas would you like to grow?

Answering this question honestly will provide accountability for members of the group. Encourage them to go one step further and identify specific steps they will take to grow in the area(s) they identify.

> **Optional activity:** Direct group members to complete the activity "Pray, Care, Share" on page 29. As time permits, encourage volunteers to share their responses.

Note: The following question does not appear in the group member book. Use it in your group discussion as time allows.

QUESTION 6: When have you seen practical love result in spiritual fruit?

This question requires group members to interact with the biblical text from this session and then respond with a personal story based on their interpretation.

LIVE IT OUT

Encourage group members to consider the following suggestions for how they can actively and intentionally show love to people this week:

- **Pray.** Take a prayer walk through your neighborhood. Pray for the spiritual, emotional, and financial needs of each household—and pray especially for their salvation.

- **Care.** Actively look for someone in need this week. Determine to give sacrificially, whether of your time, money, or other resources to help that person in the name of Jesus.

- **Share.** Think of someone you've prayed for or helped in practical ways but never talked to about Jesus. Bring Jesus into your conversation with that person. Let him or her know your concern is motivated by the love of Christ in your life.

Challenge: As members of the church, we have an opportunity to create a culture that's way more attractive than anything a corporation could produce. The suggestions in the "Live It Out" section will help you take action this week. Consider spending some additional time developing a plan for how you will cultivate love in these relationships over the long term.

Pray: Ask for prayer requests and ask group members to pray for the different requests as intercessors. As the leader, close this time by expressing your desire to demonstrate your love for God by showing love to other people. Ask God to present opportunities for the members of your group to show love to one another, and for additional opportunities for your group as a whole to demonstrate love within your community.

SESSION 4: UNSTOPPABLE OPPORTUNITIES

The Point: We intersect daily with people who need Christ.

The Passage: Acts 3:1-10

The Setting: The early Christian church in Jerusalem was comprised of Jews. Most if not all of them continued to participate in the Jewish rituals and worship. One day, as Peter and John were going up to the temple complex to take part in the afternoon hour of prayer, they encountered a lame man begging at the temple gate. They used this opportunity to demonstrate the power of Jesus Christ to this lame man and all those present at the temple.

QUESTION 1: When has a "chance" encounter changed your life?

> *Optional activity:* Prior to the group gathering, take a picture of a major intersection in your community. After discussing Question 1, pass out a wallet-sized copy of that picture to each of your group members as a reminder that all of us will intersect daily with people who need to hear the good news of Jesus Christ. Encourage group members to carry those pictures with them throughout the coming week.

Video Summary: One day, as Peter and John were going up to the temple complex to take part in the afternoon hour of prayer, they encountered a lame man begging at the temple gate. They viewed this not as an interruption but as an opportunity to demonstrate the power of Jesus Christ to this lame man and all those present at the temple. Every day we intersect with people, but we don't always take the time to notice them without simply passing by. God puts us in places to impact and influence lives along our journey.

▶ WATCH THE DVD SEGMENT FOR SESSION 4. THEN USE THE FOLLOWING QUESTIONS AND DISCUSSION POINTS TO TRANSITION INTO THE STUDY.

- Do you more often tend to view people as scenery, machinery, or ministry? Explain.
- What will you do this week to seize opportunities rather than view them as distractions?

WHAT DOES THE BIBLE SAY?
▶ ASK FOR A VOLUNTEER TO READ ALOUD ACTS 3:1-10.

Response: What's your initial reaction to these verses?

- What do you like about the text?
- What new application do you hope to receive about how intersections can become opportunities?

▶ TURN THE GROUP'S ATTENTION TO ACTS 3:1-4.

QUESTION 2: How can we get better at noticing the opportunities God gives us to love others?

This question is intended to help group members make the connection between recognizing opportunities to love others and our responsibility in positioning ourselves to act on those opportunities.

> *Optional follow-up:* What emotions do you experience when God interrupts your day?

▶ MOVE TO ACTS 3:5-8.

QUESTION 3: When have you seen Jesus make a dramatic difference in someone's life?

This question invites members of the group to share stories of how they have personally witnessed the power of Jesus making a dramatic difference in someone's life.

> *Optional activity:* Direct group members to complete the activity "Community Intersections" on page 35. If time allows, encourage volunteers to share their responses.

▶ CONTINUE WITH ACTS 3:9-10.

QUESTION 4: How have you been affected personally by others' obedience to Christ?

As in question 3, this question gives group members an opportunity to share from personal experience.

> *Optional follow-up:* When have you felt led to care for someone in need as a result of the obedience of others?

QUESTION 5: How can we make room now so we can say yes to future opportunities to serve?

This is an application question included to encourage group members to share action steps. It promotes accountability and the need to act on biblical principles.

> *Optional follow-up:* What is our role in creating opportunities to meet needs and share the gospel?

Note: The following question does not appear in the group member book. Use it in your group discussion as time allows.

QUESTION 6: What obstacles have prevented you from seeking out opportunities to share the gospel in your everyday life?

Answering this question requires group members to examine the things in their own lives that have kept them from seeking opportunities to share the gospel. Remind them that they aren't alone as you encourage their honesty.

LIVE IT OUT

Invite group members to consider the following suggestions for making the most of the intersections and opportunities that come their way this week:

- **Look.** Search for such opportunities. Allow your schedule to be interrupted in order to minister by listening, offering encouragement, praying with someone, or meeting a need.

- **Go for it.** Take the steps of obedience that you've been putting off recently. Take a leap of faith and do what you know God has been calling you to do.

- **Sign up.** You don't have to wait for opportunities to fall in your lap through the regular intersections of life. Consider talking with a staff person at your church and signing up for ministry opportunities that match your gifts.

Challenge: To follow Jesus is to serve a sovereign God—a God familiar with every nuance of your life and the lives of others. That doesn't leave much room for random chance. Think about the intersections and opportunities that have made a difference in your life. Spend time this week thanking God for these.

Pray: Ask for prayer requests and ask group members to pray for the different requests as intercessors. As the leader, conclude by confessing that you have missed opportunities in recent months to intersect with people in a meaningful way. Reaffirm your desire—as an individual and as a member of your group—to make the most of the seemingly random encounters God brings your way each day.

SESSION 5: UNSTOPPABLE COURAGE

The Point: God gives us courage to speak boldly for Christ.

The Passage: Acts 4:1-3,8-12,19-20

The Setting: Peter and John encountered a lame beggar on their way to the Jerusalem temple at the afternoon hour of prayer. In the name of Jesus Christ the man was healed. Peter used the opportunity to preach the gospel to those present in the temple. The Jewish religious leaders were offended by Peter and John teaching the people in the temple and proclaiming Jesus' resurrection from the dead. They arrested Peter and John, bringing them before the assembled Jewish leadership to answer for their words and actions.

QUESTION 1: What's the most courageous act you've ever seen?

> *Optional activity:* Supplement your group's discussion of Question 1 by playing one or more video clips of people acting courageously. These clips could include fictional situations from movies and TV shows or real-life videos of people being courageous—or a mixture of both.

Video Summary: Peter and John did a good deed that drew attention to Jesus Christ, and that got them in hot water with the religious leaders who opposed them. The Jewish religious leaders arrested Peter and John, bringing them before the assembled Jewish leadership to answer for their words and actions. Peter and John were compelled—unstoppable—in speaking about Jesus. God gives us courage to stand strong in the face of adversity. Unstoppable courage is stepping out of our comfort zone and stepping into the freedom of being tethered to Jesus.

▶ WATCH THE DVD SEGMENT FOR SESSION 5. THEN USE THE FOLLOWING QUESTIONS AND DISCUSSION POINTS TO TRANSITION INTO THE STUDY.

- ● Who do you consider to be courageous? Why?
- ● Do you feel like a courageous person? Explain.

WHAT DOES THE BIBLE SAY?

▶ ASK FOR A VOLUNTEER TO READ ALOUD ACTS 4:1-3,8-12,19-20.

Response: What's your initial reaction to these verses?

- ● What questions do you have about these verses?
- ● What new application do you hope to get from this passage?

▶ TURN THE GROUP'S ATTENTION TO ACTS 4:1-3.

QUESTION 2: What are the risks we face when we proclaim the gospel?

This question will help group members understand the barriers they have experienced personally in choosing to share the gospel message with others.

> ***Optional follow-up:*** What are some ways people in our culture express their discomfort with the gospel?

> ***Optional activity:*** Direct group members to complete the activity "Picturing Courage" on page 43. As time allows, encourage volunteers to share which image they picked and why.

▶ MOVE TO ACTS 4:8-12.

QUESTION 3: In a culture that values tolerance above all, how do we boldly and lovingly communicate the message of verse 12?

This question requires members to interpret the biblical text and then look beyond the words of the passage to discover what can be learned about how we can best communicate the truth of salvation in our culture today.

> ***Optional follow-up:*** When have you had an opportunity to speak boldly about Jesus?

QUESTION 4: How would you describe the role of the Holy Spirit in sharing the gospel?

This question is intended to lead group members to identify what they can know about the role of the Holy Spirit based on the words of this biblical text.

▶ CONTINUE WITH ACTS 4:19-20.

QUESTION 5: Where is God directing your group to demonstrate a greater level of courage?

This question will give group members an opportunity to examine, through the filter of the biblical text, where they may be feeling called to be more courageous. Encourage them to collaborate rather than answer the question individually.

> ***Optional follow-up:*** How can we discern whether we're trying to please God or please people?

Note: The following question does not appear in the group member book. Use it in your group discussion as time allows.

QUESTION 6: What steps can we take to support one another in speaking boldly about Jesus in our community?

This question provides group members with an opportunity to identify practical steps toward positive action. Try to steer them away from talking theory; encourage them to get practical.

> ***Optional follow-up:*** In what ways do you now feel better equipped to speak boldly about Jesus?

LIVE IT OUT

Encourage group members to consider the following options for how they will demonstrate courage as they follow Christ this week:

- **Please God.** At the end of each day, evaluate your actions and attitudes by answering this question: "Whom did I live to please today?" Practice becoming a God-pleaser rather than a people-pleaser.

- **Read up.** Information is a great complement to courage. To better understand why Jesus is the only way to heaven, read *Jesus Among Other Gods: The Absolute Claims of the Christian Message* by Ravi Zacharias (W Publishing, 2002).

- **Take action.** Do some research and find a place in your community or state where the gospel is being silenced. Take action to get that policy changed: write to a government official, attend a public meeting and voice your opinion, start a petition, or join a group that works to correct the wrong.

Challenge: Christians in America and other Western cultures are fortunate that we don't often find ourselves prohibited from sharing the gospel. We can still demonstrate the courage that has defined so many believers for so long. How will you demonstrate unstoppable courage this week?

Pray: Ask for prayer requests and ask group members to pray for the different requests as intercessors. As the leader, close this time by praising God for the many positive examples contained in the Scriptures, including the stories of Peter and John. Ask for the courage and strength of mind necessary to continue the work of spreading the gospel that began with the early church.

SESSION 6: UNSTOPPABLE IMPACT

The Point: The gospel of Jesus Christ can impact any culture.

The Passage: Acts 17:16-18,22-23,30-31

The Setting: During Paul's second missionary journey, in answer to a vision, Paul and his companions brought the gospel to Macedonia and into Europe for the first time. After visiting Philippi, Thessalonica, and Berea, Paul traveled to Athens. While waiting for his companions Silas and Timothy to join him, Paul spent his time preaching the gospel to the people of Athens—to the Jews in the synagogue, the general populace and the philosophers in the marketplace, and the leadership at the Areopagus.

QUESTION 1: What do you enjoy most about different cultures?

> *Optional activity:* Supplement your group's discussion of Question 1 by making travel brochures and books available at the beginning of your gathering. Make sure to bring books and brochures that highlight different cultures around the world, and encourage group members to glance through them as they discuss what they like best about different cultures.

Video Summary: In Acts 17, Paul gave us an example of communicating the gospel in a diverse culture. America is a very diverse country: cultures, ethnicities, worldviews, and preferences. It is our human nature to gravitate toward people who are more like ourselves, but the beauty of the gospel is that it is not only for people "just like me." The gospel speaks to any culture, any time, and any place. We need to build a bridge from Christ to culture and from culture to Christ. God wants to use us to build bridges and relationships with others.

▶ WATCH THE DVD SEGMENT FOR SESSION 6. THEN USE THE FOLLOWING QUESTIONS AND DISCUSSION POINTS TO TRANSITION INTO THE STUDY.

- What are the bridges you can build?
- How might God want to use your small group to build bridges to others?

WHAT DOES THE BIBLE SAY?

▶ ASK FOR A VOLUNTEER TO READ ALOUD ACTS 17:16-18,22-23,30-31.

Response: What's your initial reaction to these verses?

- What questions do you have about what it means to impact our culture with the gospel of Christ?
- What new application do you hope to get from this passage?

▶ TURN THE GROUP'S ATTENTION TO ACTS 17:16-18.

QUESTION 2: What are the cultures and subcultures in your community?

This question will give group members an opportunity to intentionally consider who surrounds them in their community and who they may have a chance to impact for the kingdom.

> *Optional follow-up:* In what ways is our culture similar to and different from the one Paul visited in Athens?

> *Optional activity:* Direct group members to complete the activity "Building Bridges" on page 51. If time permits, encourage volunteers to share their responses.

▶ MOVE TO ACTS 17:22-23.

QUESTION 3: What principles and practices can we gain from Paul's approach to sharing the gospel?

This question is designed to help group members actively engage the Scripture text and then interpret, in their own words, what application can be gained.

> *Optional follow-up:* How can we use the things we have in common with others as a gateway to sharing Jesus?

▶ CONTINUE WITH ACTS 17:30-31.

QUESTION 4: Why are so many Christians comfortable with remaining silent?

This question is designed to help group members consider things that can get in the way of speaking up. Answers will vary based on individual experiences.

> *Optional follow-up:* What are some of the ways we rationalize our silence when we miss opportunities to share the gospel?

QUESTION 5: How can our group engage one or more of the cultures in our community?

This question is associated with building biblical community. Developing an action plan as a group creates connection and accountability among the members. Belonging to redemptive community is an important aspect of being part of an unstoppable impact.

> *Optional follow-up:* What steps do you need to take as an individual to help your group successfully engage your community?

Note: The following question does not appear in the group member book. Use it in your group discussion as time allows.

QUESTION 6: What opportunities already exist through our church for spreading the gospel to different cultures in our community?

This question provides group members with an opportunity to identify practical steps for positive actions based on opportunities that are already available to them. Try to steer them away from talking theory; encourage them to get practical.

LIVE IT OUT

We have an imperative to take the gospel to the world, but the nations have also come to us. Encourage group members to consider the following steps they can take to be better prepared:

- **Get educated.** Learn about the different cultures of the people in your community. Ask about their customs, heritage, and beliefs. Attend an ethnic festival or performance. Become a student of different cultures in an effort to start discussions.

- **Get spiritual.** Follow Paul's example by attending a worship service within a different culture. Seek out common ground in order to build bridges between that culture and Christ.

- **Get official.** Talk with a staff person at your church about forming a ministry outreach to serve the different cultures in your community.

Challenge: As the world becomes more diverse, we will encounter different cultures, ethnicities, worldviews, and preferences in everyday life. That's not a problem; it's an opportunity. The question for you is: *How will you use that opportunity?* Spend some time this week thinking about specific, practical actions you can take.

Pray: As the leader, close this final session of *Unstoppable Gospel* in prayer. Thank God for the privilege of studying His Word throughout this resource. Conclude the study by praising God for the impact of His unstoppable gospel throughout history and around the world. On behalf of your group, verbally proclaim your desire to join in the continued advancement of that gospel through the church.

Note: If you haven't discussed it yet, decide as a group whether or not you plan to continue to meet together and, if so, what Bible study options you would like to pursue. Visit *LifeWay.com/smallgroups* for help, or if you would like more studies like this one, visit *biblestudiesforlife.com/smallgroups.*

My group's prayer requests

ALSO AVAILABLE ...

SMALL GROUP LEADER KIT

BIBLE STUDIES FOR LIFE

CONNECTED
MY LIFE IN THE CHURCH

THOM S. RAINER

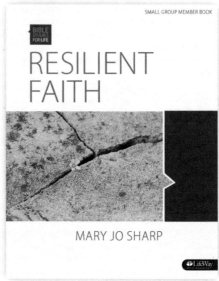

SMALL GROUP MEMBER BOOK

BIBLE STUDIES FOR LIFE

RESILIENT FAITH

MARY JO SHARP

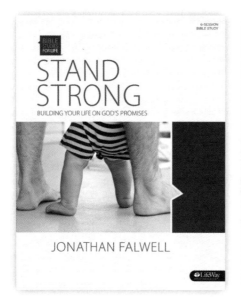

6-SESSION BIBLE STUDY

BIBLE STUDIES FOR LIFE

STAND STRONG
BUILDING YOUR LIFE ON GOD'S PROMISES

JONATHAN FALWELL

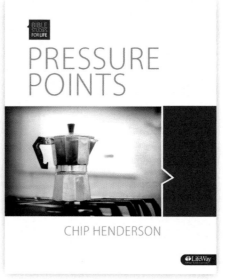

BIBLE STUDIES FOR LIFE

PRESSURE POINTS

CHIP HENDERSON

BIBLE STUDIES FOR LIFE®

This series helps people understand how to apply the Bible to everyday life—their families, their careers, and their struggles—just as they are, right where they live. A new study releases every three months.

Discover available studies at
biblestudiesforlife.com/smallgroups,
800.458.2772, or at your **LifeWay Christian Store**.